RISING ABOVE

RISING ABOVE

The Early Years of
Mario Cervelli

KEITH JOHNSON

iUniverse, Inc.
New York   Bloomington

Rising Above
The Early Years of Mario Cervelli

iUniverse books may be ordered through booksellers or by contacting:
iUniverse
1663 Liberty Drive
Bloomington, IN 47403
www.iuniverse.com
1-800-Authors (1-800-288-4677)

Cover Photos: Paul Lewis, Helena, Montana

The two Italy maps (pages 4 and 72) are licensed under the Creative Commons Attribution-Share Alike 3.0 Unported License. To view a copy of this license, visit http://creativecommons.org/licenses/by-sa/3.0/ or send a letter to Creative Commons, 171 Second Street, Suite 300, San Francisco, California, 94105, USA. It is a derivative file from the following: Author: NuclearVacuum File: Location European nation states.svg. These maps, made by Keith Johnson, added the place names to the maps and made them grayscale maps.

The quote on pages vi and 90 is from: Booker T. Washington, Up From Slavery: An Autobiography (New York: A.L. Burt Company 1901), p. 39.

The quote on page 76 is from Joseph Conrad, A Personal Record (New York and London: Harper and Brothers Publishers, 1912), p. 12.

ISBN: 978-1-4502-4185-4 (sc)
ISBN: 978-1-4502-4186-1 (ebk)

Printed in the United States of America
iUniverse rev. date: 9/07/2010

To Mario

"I have learned that success is to be measured not so much by the position that one has reached in life as by the obstacles which he has overcome while trying to succeed."

Booker T. Washington

Contents

Preface

For years, family members and friends of Mario Cervelli heard these stories and recognized the need for them to be preserved. In a very personal way, I desire that my children, grandchildren, and future generations have access to these family treasures.

This book tells Mario's story from his birth in Temu (pronounced teh **moo)**, Italy, in 1926, until he was 23 years old and working in Helena (pronounced **hel** luh nuh), Montana, United States of America.

I sat down with Mario for many hours over the course of several months and simply asked him to tell me his stories. I asked follow-up questions as we talked, gaining further insights. In addition, I investigated the parts of his story which fascinated me; for example, the confinement of Italian prisoners of war at Fort Missoula in Montana.

One can legitimately question the accuracy of his recollection of events that happened sixty to eighty years ago. Several times during the preparation of this manuscript, I sought to verify what Mario told me. In my research, I found that historical records verified his accounts. He remembered not only the name of a golf opponent, but also the correct spelling. His memory of a certain Notre Dame football game was accurate, even to the point of knowing the day of the week, the date, the opponent, the coach, and the correct score. Mario has excellent recall of the events in his early years.

Finally, I have documented and illustrated the events with historical and recent photographs, official documents, newspaper clippings, and personal artifacts, most of which are from albums or scrapbooks kept by Mario and his sister Frances. Mario was always ready to lend a hand in providing access to these historical treasures.

Acknowledgements

Members of my writing group have been supportive, encouraging, and critically helpful. For their faithful companionship in this journey, I want to thank Stan Lynde, Sean Connolly, Ida Meyers, Dana Holzer, and Victoria Foster.

Thank you also to Margaret Liles and Barbara Gallagher for providing valuable insights in the editing process of the book.

Further, thank you to The Historical Museum of Fort Missoula, in Missoula, Montana, for allowing me to photograph the items donated by Mario Cervelli to the Museum and helping me understand that part of the story.

Finally, thank you to my wife Nina and to my daughters Maria and Grace, who have been the inspiration for the book and provided the support necessary to make it happen.

A Hero's Welcome

As he stepped off the bus into the dark, he wondered where he should go. Usually not much happened at midnight in a small town in the mountains of northern Italy. That night was no exception. Casually walking up the main street, going nowhere in particular, he came to a large fountain spouting fresh water in the town square. Thirsty, he cupped his hands and took a drink.

The nineteen-year-old private first class American soldier, wearing his uniform, was pondering his next steps when a young man approached.

"Excuse me," the soldier began. The young Italian recognized him immediately, but not because he had ever met him or even seen him before. Instead, he knew the American because word had spread throughout the town to watch for one of their own who was coming home.

"Do you know where my aunt lives?" the soldier asked. He didn't know if his aunt had moved and was afraid that he might knock on the door of a stranger in the middle of the night.

The young man directed him up the hill and through the winding cobblestone streets to a light brown stucco-and-stone house where the soldier's aunt lived. She enthusiastically welcomed him despite the late hour, and they reminisced together, speaking in Italian, into the night. By the next morning, a Sunday, the town knew the local boy had come home.

When word of the return came to the soldier's uncle, he quickly went to his sister's house and warmly kissed and embraced his nephew. As they walked together to attend mass at the church, and later throughout the town, the uncle proudly introduced the soldier, not unlike a little boy showing off his new toy. The uncle's pride wasn't simply about family ties; his nephew was a part of the Allied Forces that had helped liberate Italy. It was a hero's welcome.

The return of the soldier coincided with the annual day of celebration for St. Bartholomew, the patron saint of this small Italian village. At the big town feast later in the day, the private became reacquainted with people with whom he had played in the streets, labored in the fields, worshipped at the church, and survived hardships before he had left some nine years earlier.

He was home. Reflecting that night, lying in a bed in his aunt's house, he considered the journey that had led him to that moment.

Map of Italy

Temu

Located some one hundred and twenty miles northeast of Milan, Italy's second largest city, the town of Temu sits nestled among the spectacular Italian Alps. Today, in the summertime, the people of Milan, *Milanesi,* and other Europeans flock to Temu, a town of approximately 1,000 residents, to escape the heat. In the wintertime, they come to ski, right from the town or up the road about nine miles on Tonale Pass, where they can ski year-round on a glacier.

Temu was a different community in 1926. With two grocery stores, a post office, a school, and a church, Temu was a farming community of perhaps 450 people. While the town had electricity, water came from a communal fountain. The farm work was all done by hand and children were required to help in the fields. Families cut the hay with crude cutters, hauled it in carts pulled by cows, and stacked it in barns. They planted potatoes one by one and dug them up the same way. They harvested and thrashed wheat as families. The Italian government dictated where firewood could be cut for the winter supply, and families cut the wood, hauled it into town, and stacked it.

Most families relied on the forests to provide food in the form of wildlife, berries, and mushrooms. In addition, many families raised one pig for meat and owned two cows to help work the land and to provide milk. In the evening, people in Temu milked their cows, brought the milk to a central area, weighed it, recorded the weight, and poured it into wooden tubs which were then lowered into the cold stream running through town. In a sort of town cooperative, taking turns once a month, each family would use the milk to make butter and cheese.

It was here in Temu, on July 13, 1926, that Mario Bonino Cervelli, the son of Cesare and Freda Cervelli, began his life. Because Mario was born two months premature, Freda placed her new son in a shoebox next to the wood stove to keep him warm.

Mario's family often ate the same menu and never wasted anything. Polenta (cornmeal) with rabbit stew for dinner became fried polenta or polenta in milk for breakfast. A pot of vegetable soup was warmed up again for the next meal. Mario literally roasted chestnuts on an open fire to provide tasty treats for his family.

Being poor meant improvising when it came to shoes and slippers. The Cervellis would look for rags and cut out of them the shape of each child's feet, making five pairs of shapes. Mario would then sew the five pieces of cloth together to form the sole of his slipper and women would sew tops onto the soles. Work in the fields required something sturdier, so they carved pieces of wood to fit the size of their feet and nailed pieces of cloth or leather across the top.

Mario went to school in Temu until the fifth grade. In small classes, with many ages combined, school was about academics. Athletics and extracurricular activities were not a part of school life.

Mario (second row, left) with classmates and teacher, Miss Donati, in Temu

Often when school was not in session, Mario went to visit his great uncle, Domenico, a sheepherder who lived in the mountains during the summer months taking care of other people's sheep and goats. The herds roamed at higher elevations to graze in order to save lower pastures for winter.

At the time of Mario's childhood, Benito Mussolini was the Prime Minister and dictator in Italy. Called *Il Duce,* he consolidated all power, with himself as the leader of the Italian Fascist Party, to which all teachers in schools and universities had to swear allegiance. While historically many fascist governments have sprung up, fascism began with Mussolini. Despite the fact that most definitions of fascism place an emphasis on a strong dictator, Mario recalls being taught that the focus of fascism was not on the individual but on the group, or the "bundle." The symbol of fascism, imprinted on the cover of his elementary school books, was a bundle with a protruding ax head. He was clearly taught that if Italians were going to advance as a people, it would happen as a result of putting the state first, bundling together, so that they would all get ahead.

Benito Mussolini

Mario's elementary school book
The symbol on the cover of the book was the symbol
for Mussolini's fascist government.

LA MARCIA SU ROMA.

A page from the school book

Mussolini also established the *Opera Nazionale Balilla*, a youth organization, to indoctrinate young Italians in what it meant to be fascist and Italian. Mario became a member when he was eight, proudly wearing his arm band and military hat. He carried his membership card with the following pledge in Italian:

> *"In the name of God and of Italy, I swear to honor the orders of the Duce (Mussolini) to serve with all my force and, if necessary, also with my blood, for the cause of the fascist revolution." [Mario's translation]*

Mario's Opera Nazionale Balilla membership card

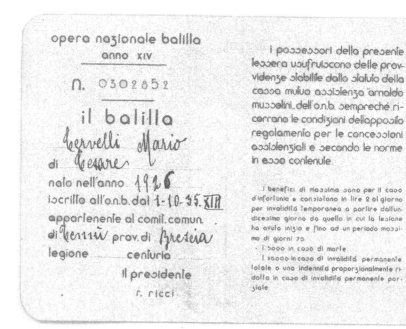

Mario's Opera Nazionale Balilla membership card

When Mussolini gave speeches to his country, the people of Temu gathered in the town square to listen to the radio, the only one in Temu, broadcast over a loudspeaker.

While life in Temu was mostly about hard work, periodic events broke the routine. In the winter, Temu developed into a ski retreat. Some locals, along with others from out of town, joined the many downhill and cross-country ski clubs. Mario, however, was not one of them because he didn't have skis and wasn't particularly interested.

Weddings created excitement for the people of Temu. They celebrated with big feasts for the whole town, and for poor children that meant cakes and candy, foods they rarely ate because their families couldn't afford them.

People anticipated the annual Catholic celebrations of Easter, Christmas, and Epiphany. At Christmas, each community in the mountains created its own nativity scene, or *crèche*. Together with the Catholic sisters in their town, the young people of Temu would walk, sometimes many miles, to the little towns of Cané, Vione, and Ponte d'Legno to view their displays.

Children were most eager, however, for Epiphany, on January 6, in which the church commemorated the arrival of the wise men, or magi, at Jesus' home. With great excitement and anticipation, children in Temu placed one of their shoes outside the door of their home, much like hanging stockings over a fireplace in the United States. They then waited for *Befana*, according to Italian folklore an old woman who filled the shoes with gifts. In the morning, with great happiness and contentment, Mario would find an orange and candy in his shoe.

Mario recalls his Confirmation as one the biggest days of his life. The Bishop of the province came to Temu, and the townspeople lined all the streets with white sheets and held a massive feast. While most of the children being confirmed had godparents who stood up for them, Mario's godfather was out of town working and couldn't attend the big event. Others had their pictures taken that day, but Mario did not.

Children in Temu learned to entertain themselves. While out in the hills watching animals, for example, the boys created their own sports. In one sport, they began by searching for sticks with a club-like end, much like a hockey stick or a golf club. They then marked out a square, digging a hole in each corner and another in the center. Placing a ball in the middle, they sought to hit it into their corner. At other times, the boys occupied themselves by playing marbles on the main street. Placing ten marbles in a straight line on the dirt road that ran through the town, they would try to hit each other's marbles to capture them.

These early days of Mario's life in Temu taught this poor young boy the value of hard work, the significance of family and community in one's life, the need to be thankful for even small pleasures, and the importance of loyalty, respect, and integrity.

A Pathway to America

arios grandfather had begun his life some eighteen miles south of Temu in the town of Cevo (pronounced **cheh** voh). He came to America in the mid-1800's to work in the coal mines of Starkville, Colorado. Mario's father, Cesare, was born in Colorado in 1898, which made him an American citizen.

After growing up in Colorado, Cesare accompanied his family when they moved back to Cevo. World War I broke out, and Cesare served in the Italian army. After the war, he met Fridale "Freda" Pasina, from Temu, and they married. Cesare and Freda had three children—Mario, his sister Frances, and his brother Dino.

Cesare Cervelli in World War 1

While at times Cesare worked in Temu, during the years his family was growing up, he often had jobs in other places in Europe. Laboring as a coal miner, or at any other job he could find, he worked in France, Belgium, Germany, and Switzerland.

In 1932, leading up to World War II, Europe became very uneasy and in Italy, Mussolini had become very powerful. As life for citizens grew more difficult, a friend of Cesare from North Adams, Massachusetts, wrote and reminded him that he was an American citizen. Further, he advised him to get out of Italy before he got drafted into the Italian army. Cesare gave heed to the counsel, left his family in Temu, and came to America, not knowing when there would be enough money for them to join him.

Mario, Frances, Freda, and Dino Cervelli in Temu

Cesare first went to Ballston Lake, New York, to live with Freda's uncle and look for a job. Because of the Great Depression in America at the time, however, Cesare couldn't find employment and wrote to his wife telling her the bad news.

Cesare Cervelli (right) with a friend in Ballston Lake, New York

Back in Italy, Freda became increasingly concerned. One day, while she was visiting in a nearby town, a friend introduced her to a woman who was about to be married. As they were talking, Freda shared how she was alone with her children and that her husband was in America unable to find work.

The lady said, "Well, my fiancé is in America. I'm planning to go there soon to get married." Following up on the conversation, this young lady wrote to her fiancé in America, passing on what she had learned about the woman from Temu. Freda's husband, however, was in New York and the fiancé of the young bride-to-be was in Montana. Upon receiving the letter, the man wrote to his fiancée asking her to tell Freda to write to her husband and instruct him to come to Montana, where a job was waiting for him.

**Helena, Montana, and Ballston Lake, New York,
are about 2,300 miles apart.**

Soon the important letter arrived in New York with the good news. Cesare said good-bye to his hosts and took a train across the country to Helena, where he found that fiancé, John Leggerini. He immediately went to work on Leggerini's ranch, some five miles outside of town, along Ten Mile Creek.

Four years later, in 1936, Cesare finally was able to send for his family.

Leaving Temu

When the Cervelli family received word that they could join Cesare in America, they immediately prepared for their trip and their new life.

First, through the Catholic Church in Temu, they made religious preparations. The priest heard the news of the Cervellis' departure and told Freda that he wanted to be sure that the whole family had their First Communion and their Confirmation before they left because he didn't know what they would face in America. Even though technically they weren't old enough, Mario's sister Frances and brother Dino received these Catholic rites.

In addition, Freda made a promise. While her husband was living in America, the owners of a grocery store had extended credit to her for food staples like sugar, salt, and coffee. This went on for years. Even though she had no way to pay her bill at the time she left, Freda went to the store and promised that they would send money to pay their bill as soon as they were able. The woman who owned the store pessimistically replied that she would never see the money.

Mario's passport

On July 26, 1936, with passports in hand containing photos taken with the one camera in Temu, the family gathered to say good-bye. That morning Mario and Dino wore blue sailor suits with short pants. Zia Seconda, Freda's sister, was on hand to help them prepare for the trip. In an attempt to frighten the children, she jokingly said, "I'm sure glad I'm not going to America because I'd be afraid of the sharks in the ocean." As the family members parted, they understood that in saying goodbye they would probably never see each other again. (Zia Seconda was the only one of Mario's family from Temu to ever visit America, coming in 1967 and staying for six months with her sister.)

This was a time of firsts for Mario. Climbing into the only automobile owned by a person in Temu, the Cervellis left for America—Mario's first time in a car. They stopped in Edolo, some 10 miles down the mountains, and boarded a train to southern Italy—Mario's first time on a train. After traveling some 525 miles, they arrived in the port city of Naples to await their ship. Finally, on July 30, the Cervellis climbed aboard the transatlantic ocean liner, Rex—Mario's first time on a boat as well.

The Rex

LIST OR MANIFEST OF ALIEN PASSENGERS FOR THE UNITED

S.S. *REX*, Passengers sailing from NAPLES, JULY 9th, 1936

The Rex passenger manifest
Mario's age is listed incorrectly.

Mario and his family marveled as they walked onto one of the premier luxury liners of its day. In addition to its beauty, the Rex was fast, having become, in 1933, the holder of the *Blue Riband* for the fastest Atlantic Ocean crossing. People chose the Rex for its extravagant amenities—fine food, a swimming pool, deluxe cabins, and ornate Art Deco styling. The great food included ice cream, again a first for Mario.

Staircase on the Rex

The Cervellis' third-class cabin had four beds; while their room was in the bottom of the boat, they came up onto the deck often. Looking out at the ocean through the rails, at times they saw schools of dolphin jumping in the waves. Walking to the front of the Rex, Mario would lie on his stomach, his head hanging over the edge of the ship, to watch fish jump as the bow sliced through the water.

As fascinated as he was with these simple pleasures, however, he wondered where this beautiful ship was taking him and what his new life would be like.

A New Beginning

As the Rex slowly maneuvered into the harbor in New York City, the young boy from Italy looked at the tall buildings and thought, "This place is out of this world." Along with hundreds of other passengers, the family disembarked at Ellis Island and immigration officials guided them through a health inspection. Because of Cesare's United States citizenship, as well as the fact that he was employed and established in Montana, his family quickly received permission to enter the country.

Immediately boarding a train, the Cervellis left New York. On August 9, 1936, they arrived at the Great Northern Depot in Helena, Montana, where Cesare met his wife and children after a four-year separation.

The reunited family headed to Leggerini's ranch west of Helena and moved into a small cabin which originally had been a trolley car in the city of Helena. It had been converted into living quarters consisting of two small rooms, with no electricity or running water. Water came from a nearby well which was simply a hole in the ground. Family members would lower a bucket into the hole to retrieve water for drinking and bathing. Kerosene lamps were their only source of indoor light, and a wood stove stood in one room and provided the only heat. In winter, the windows frosted over with ice, while in summer, the sun made the little cabin stifling hot.

The Cervellis' cabin

You can see the outline of the trolley car in this view of the cabin.

Leggerini's metal barn as it looks today

John Leggerini was a typical Italian person living in Helena, described as "very thrifty" or "very tight," depending on who was making the comment. Workers on the ranch toiled long and hard hours, including Leggerini's niece, who cooked for everyone. Leggerini's main crops were hay, which he sold throughout the winter to provide food for other people's animals, and potatoes, which were purchased by local stores. In addition, he raised pigs, usually butchered by Cesare and sold to local markets. In the summer, Helenans came to the ranch to purchase strawberries, which they had to pick themselves from a two-acre patch.

While Cesare was officially the hired hand, Mario also got involved with the work on the ranch. Mario recalls fondly how in the summertime, after a long day of work, he and his father would walk together after dinner to a small pump house a few hundred yards away on the side of the road and turn on the irrigation system for the potatoes.

Leggerini's pump house as it looks today

While living on the ranch, Freda could have been described as a stay-at-home mom. She cared for her children, making sure they went to school and did well in their studies. In addition, she performed all of the manual household chores required by living in a small cabin with few amenities.

Mario was also involved in the control of pests on the ranch. Gopher holes posed a constant threat because cows could break their legs when they stepped into them. To combat the gopher problem, Leggerini hired Mario and Dino to become exterminators. Environmental concerns were low on the priority list back then, so armed with a bucket of oats that had been combined with poison, they went out into the fields regularly in the morning and placed a spoonful of the mixture at the mouth of each gopher hole. Later, in the afternoon, they would return to gather up all the dead pests. Bringing the harvest to Leggerini, they were paid five cents for each gopher. Because the boys were so desperate for money, Leggerini wanted to be sure that the brothers wouldn't return the next day with the same animals. He simply threw the poison-laden varmints into Ten Mile Creek where they were washed downstream.

One day when Mario visited a neighbor up the creek, the owner of the ranch walked up the bank with a tub which held perhaps ten to twenty fish. Curious, Mario asked, "How did you catch all those fish?" Again showing little concern for clean water, the rancher pointed to a pool in the creek and replied, "You see that fishing hole over there? I just threw a whole bunch of horse manure in there. Then the fish all swam up to the top and I just scooped them up with a net."

In September, one month after their arrival, the three Italian children began their American education in the one-room Baxendale Schoolhouse, up the road about a mile toward MacDonald Pass. While they had picked up a few words during their first month in the United States, including a few choice ones taught by the ranch hands, their English was very limited. Fellow students often ridiculed Mario, Frances, and Dino because of their inability to communicate.

The Baxendale Schoolhouse as it looks today

That year, their teacher, Miss Helen Mulligan, was fresh from teacher training, beginning her first teaching assignment. She used to say, "I will never forget my first day of school and how they brought me three children who didn't even speak the language." Even though the school never offered classes in English, the Cervelli children picked up the language through everyday learning at school and day-to-day life at home.

While Mario was an average student, his report cards from his first years of school clearly indicate that he excelled in art and music.

Mario with the students of Baxendale School
Front row: Bobby Kroll, Dino Cervelli, Donny Kroll, Johnny Kroll
Middle row: Eddie (last name unknown), David Mattice, Alice Kroll,
Betty Mattice, Frances Cervelli
Top row: Ann Clausen, Melvin Kroll, Mario Cervelli, Joanne Mattice

Mario with the boys from his school

PARENTS OR GUARDIANS PLEASE READ

At the close of each six-week period this report will be filled out by the teacher and sent to you for inspection. If your child is not making satisfactory progress you are kindly urged to consult with the teacher in an effort to secure better results. The efforts of the school and home must be closely linked in order to secure the best educational progress of the child.

If a pupil receives F on any subject, it should be made a matter of immediate inquiry. Possibly it is to be attributed to lack of study, or too many outside engagements, to irregularities in attendance or to some cause which may be removed.

Special attention is called to the serious consequences of irregular attendance. It is important to remember that the loss of even a portion of a school session often proves to be a serious interruption of progress, which tends to produce a lack of interest in the school work.

We suggest that you talk over this report with your child each time it is received, and if it has any peculiar needs which are indicated to you by the marks on this card, that you confer with the teacher regarding it.

If the parents could show their interest in the child and school by occasional visits to the school, it would prove a great source of inspiration and help to both pupil and teacher.

Your hearty cooperation is solicited in the endeavor to secure the best development of your child.

FRANCES G. FORGY,
County Superintendent of Schools.

CERTIFICATE OF PROMOTION

I CERTIFY that...................

Is { retained in grade...............
    { eligible to promotion to........
    Bettie Mae Johnson
    Teacher.

LEWIS AND CLARK COUNTY

Rural Schools

SIX - WEEK PERIOD AND ANNUAL REPORT

of *Mario Cervelli*

Grade *six*; School *Baxendale*

for the School Year *1939 - 1940*

Helen Mulligan, Teacher
Bettie M. Johnson

Parent or Guardian is requested to examine this report carefully, each page, and to acknowledge its receipt by signing below. Kindly return at once.

SIGNATURE OF PARENT OR GUARDIAN

1st Period *Cesare Cervelli*
2nd Period *Cesare Cervelli*
3rd Period *Cesare Cervelli*
4th Period *Cesare Cervelli*
5th Period *Cesare Cervelli*
5th Period

Mario's 1939–40 report card

Mario's 1939–40 report card

The children walked to the Baxendale School. When teacher
Betty Johnson came to the school, she gave Mario the responsibility
of starting the fire in the wood stove to warm up the classroom,
which required him to arrive first. For his efforts he received a
quarter a week.

Students with teacher, Miss Betty Johnson
Front row: Melvin Kroll, David Mattice, Donny Kroll, Dino Cervelli,
Howard Clausen, Mario Cervelli, Johnny Kroll, Bobby Kroll
Second row: Alice Kroll, Ann Clausen, Joanne Mattice,
Frances Cervelli, Betty Lou Mattice, Betty Johnson

Mario's perfect attendance award, May, 1938

Mario's artwork, 1941

Betty Johnson was a cousin of the legendary actress Myrna Loy. Born in Radersburg, Montana, some 40 miles southeast of Helena, Loy moved with her family to Helena where she danced on the stage of the old Marlow Theatre. After her father died, when she was thirteen, she moved with the rest of her family to Los Angeles, where she soon began her acting career. As Mario and his classmates played at recess one day, Myrna Loy came to the school to see where her cousin taught.

Myrna Loy's mother, Actress Myrna Loy,
Mario's teacher, Betty Johnson, Ann Clausen

Outside of school and work, Mario often headed out from the ranch with his buddies, all carrying their guns. Mario's rifle was a Mossberg .22, with a seven-shot clip, which he had purchased with his own money, ten dollars, after saving for a long time. They also carried the three essential provisions necessary for a day-long hunting outing—coffee, salt, and sugar. When they arrived at their destination in the hills, they would go out to hunt cottontail rabbits. After the kill, they would head back to their camp and build a fire, skin the rabbit, put it on a skewer, salt it, and roast it over the fire. To complete the feast, they would make coffee by boiling water in a can over the fire and adding the coffee and sugar.

Friends told Mario and Dino that they could earn some money at the Pine Hills Golf Course, which was located across the road toward MacDonald Pass. Prominent citizens of Helena gathered regularly at the eighteen-hole regulation course with sand greens. The young boys ended up spending their whole summer caddying for attorneys, dentists, doctors, lawyers, and even Bishop Gilmore of the Cathedral of St. Helena. Caddies earned seventy-five cents for eighteen holes, and on good days, usually on weekends, they caddied for thirty-six holes.

Caddies also got to play at Pine Hills, and Mario became a good young golfer. The Caddies' Tournament at the end of the season proved his skill. The match play competition paired Mario with his brother in an early round, and Mario won. In the final match against Sid Dalin, Mario won the club's Caddies' Championship. For his efforts, Pine Hills awarded him the grand prize of a golf bag, three balls, and a set of clubs consisting of a driver, a spoon (similar to a three wood), a five and a seven iron, and a putter.

Mario Cervelli Is Caddy Champ at Pine Hills Course

The Helena Town and Country club crowned Mario Cervelli its new caddy champion yesterday at the Pine Hills course.

Cervelli won the championship match from Sid Dalin, 7 and 6. His one-stroke handicap was not needed to win.

The new champion will be awarded a complete set of golf clubs for his efforts. Club members made donations to purchase him the prize.

Joe Flynn and Dick Carstensen will play for top honors in the first flight.

Newspaper article about Mario winning the Caddy Championship
The handwritten label on the article is incorrect.
Source: *Helena Independent*, Helena, Montana

Mario first understood community as a local value, gaining that insight in rural Italy and Montana. Building on that early understanding, he came to see community as a national value as well. Although still a young teen during the early years of World War II, Mario, as well as the people of Helena as a whole, energetically participated in the war effort. Scouring the hillsides, Mario searched for scrap iron, old tires, copper wire, aluminum, or anything that could help fight the war. On Saturdays, they would bring their recyclable goods to the big drive in downtown Helena to help fight Hitler and Mussolini, to whom he had pledged an oath earlier in life. No one was paid for what they brought. Good citizens just did that during a war. It was part of being a community.

A New Challenge

Cesare continued to work on the ranch until 1939 when he became very ill, complaining of constant headaches. He went to several local doctors but received no conclusive diagnosis. Finally, traveling by train and accompanied by his friend Scottie Palmer, he sought treatment at the Mayo Clinic in Rochester, Minnesota. At the clinic, doctors found a tumor on his brain, which they surgically removed. Cesare remained there for about a month.

Such medical treatment was expensive, and the Cervellis were without personal resources. The money for the train trip and medical treatment came from friends who rallied around the family during the illness. Many of the friends were wealthy people for whom Mario had caddied at the Pine Hills Golf Course. Art Nelson, a local banker, organized the effort to collect money. The Cervellis considered themselves very fortunate and were extremely grateful.

Freda and Mario in Helena

Despite the efforts at Mayo Clinic, when Cesare returned to Helena, he was still very ill and required constant medical treatment. As a fifteen-year-old without a driver's license, Mario drove his father to town from the ranch each morning at 9:00 for x-ray or radiation treatments at St. Peter's Hospital, located downtown on 11th Avenue. In helping his father, he often missed school.

In his last two years of life, Cesare required hospitalization many times at various medical institutions in town, including St. Peter's Hospital, St. John's Hospital, and the County Hospital, usually staying several days and then returning to the ranch. While he performed some physical labor on the ranch and also worked at the golf course from time to time, he grew weaker and weaker and eventually ceased all work. Leggerini told the family they would have to leave the ranch.

For a short time the Cervellis lived up the road about a half mile in a small log cabin on the neighboring ranch. Later they moved to another ranch, closer to MacDonald Pass, on the other side of the road, right next to the golf course. They rented a small cabin in the summer, and when the golf course closed for the winter, they became live-in caretakers of the clubhouse.

The neighboring ranch

The summer cabin

A column, "The Prospector In Last Chance Gulch," by Del Leeson, recounted the Cervellis' story. It appeared on Sunday, October 1, 1939, in the *Helena Independent*, the name of the publication before it merged with the *Montana Herald-Record* in 1943 to become the *Independent Record*. The article is presented here as it was written.

If you go out to the Helena Town and Country club today to play a bit of golf you will find a couple of youngsters by the name of Deano and Mario hanging around waiting to do some caddying for you. Everybody knows them as Deano and Mario although there are quite a few people who do not know which is Deano and which is Mario and it is very difficult to find someone who knows their last name—which happens to be Cervelli.

* * *

Deano and Mario have been caddying around the Helena Town and Country club for quite awhile. They're not very big yet but when they first went to work two or three years ago it was a little difficult to tell which was the golf bag and which was Deano or which was Mario. They were all about the same size. But that didn't bother Deano and Mario, who pitched in and did their work with a will. Sometimes, when business was rushing, Deano—who is the smaller—would "carry double." That is, he'd carry two bags at once and when he did that it was very difficult indeed to even see Deano. Which made no difference to him as long as the money rolled in.

* * *

You can hear some interesting stories about those two boys, but our favorite is about the day Deano was caddying for a man who drove his ball into the rough. Deano went to look for it and couldn't find it. Finally he came back very dejectedly. "I'm sorry, Mister," he said, "I looked an' looked but I couldn't find your ball. But," holding out his hand, "here's five others I found out there." You don't get a caddy like that very often.

* * *

So that's the way Deano and Mario went along— just a couple of little kids that were willing to work their heads off for you and do what they thought was right. Some days they'd make two or three bucks apiece and that helped out because their father, Caesar Cervelli, had got a little farm of his own up above John Leggerini's place was finding the going pretty tough. Particularly because he never seemed to feel good any more and was suffering some terrific headaches.

* * *

Finally he went to a doctor who told him he had a brain tumor and that it's removal required the kind of an operation which could not be performed here.

* * *

And then Deano and Mario learned that lesson which all of us should learn as young as we can—that the best thing in the world you can have is a friend. And Deano and Mario had them. Some of the men at the Country club got together and decided that maybe they could afford to provide hospital treatment for Mr. Cervelli at Rochester if transportation could be arranged. Well, the transportation was arranged and through the kindness of these men (whose names we know as well as we know they would prefer to remain anonymous) Deano's and Mario's father was sent down to Rochester for the best of medical attention he could obtain.

* * *

Mr. Cervelli is back here in St. Peter's hospital now, the operation performed, and he's resting fairly well. Out at the Country club this morning Deano and Mario will be waiting around to do a bit of caddying for somebody and if it's a good day maybe they'll pick up two or three bucks apiece. But it won't make much difference, really, how many bucks they pick up today. We bet they think it's a pretty good world and that there are a lot of pretty good people in it. And there always will be—if you kinda play the game right yourself.

Source: *Helena Independent*, Helena, Montana, October 1, 1939.

Cesare died on September 20, 1941, while at the summer cabin.

Cesare Cervelli

Cesar Cerbelli Is Taken by Death

Cesar Cerbelli, a Helena resident for many years and an employe of the country club, died last night after a long illness.

Surviving are his wife, two sons, Dino and Morio, and a daughter, Frances Cerbelli, all of Helena.

The body is at the Opp and Conrad mortuary.

Mr. Cerbelli was born in Colorado. Some time ago he went to Italy to live for four or five years. He and Mrs. Cerbelli were married there and the children were born there.

Cesare Cervelli's obituary
Source: *Helena Independent,* Helena, Montana, September 21, 1941

The family gathered at the Cathedral of St. Helena for the funeral, and Cesare was buried at Resurrection Cemetery, north of Helena.

While he was fifteen at the time of his father's death, Mario had spent only about five of those years actually with his father because Cesare was working away from home.

A New Reality

By the time Christmas came around that year, the fatherless family had moved back into the Pine Hills Golf Course clubhouse as its caretakers for the winter. The club members again rallied around the family and bought a pair of skates and skis for each of the three children as Christmas gifts. On Sunday afternoons, Mario, alone, would carry his skis over to hole number three, which became his ski slope. Stepping onto the skis, he'd pull the leather straps over the toes of his boots, put his hands through the straps on his poles, and race down the hill as fast as he could. The skates were less fascinating to him, and later, because the neighbor girl wanted his skates so badly, he traded them to her for his very first camera.

Before school began the following fall, the Cervellis decided to move into town, and they found a home at 714 Jackson Street. Mario started at Helena High, Frances and Dino at the Cathedral School.

Before long, however, Mario quit high school in order to provide for his family. The MacDonald Pass Dairy, some ten miles from town, hired him to help care for the cows and deliver the milk. Mario lived and worked at the dairy during the summer, beginning his days at 5:00 a.m. and often laboring until 9:00 p.m. Along with room and board, he earned fifty dollars a month, all of which he gave to his mother.

In the winter of 1943, at the age of seventeen, Mario was hired by St. John's Hospital to translate for the cooks who had moved to Helena after being released from their internment at Fort Missoula, some 120 miles away. These cooks really were first-class chefs, and they also have a fascinating story.

On December 7, 1941, the day the Japanese bombed Pearl Harbor, an Italian cruise ship staff peacefully cooked for their passengers as the ship slowly traveled through the Panama Canal. In response to the bombing, the United States confiscated the vessel and led the Italians off the ship, transporting them to an internment camp at Fort Missoula, Montana, thousands of miles away. Eventually, some 1,200 Italians ended up at the camp, which they referred to as "Camp Bella Vista," which is Italian for camp beautiful sight.

While officially prisoners, the Italians moved about with remarkable freedom in the community of Missoula and became good friends with the residents. They worked on area farms, were employed in local businesses, and fought forest fires. When the United States released them, without any money, many chose to stay in the area and begin new lives in Montana.

Italian detainees at Fort Missoula

Some of the detainees made their way east to Helena. Because these new residents had no place to live, The Great Northern Railway Company converted boxcars near the train depot into housing for the former detainees. While hardly ideal, the residents were quite comfortable despite being housed several people to a car.

While Mario translated for the chefs, his mother frequently invited them to her home for dinner. To say thank you, they gave her small tokens of appreciation. Among other things, they presented her a painting of a German shepherd dog, a small box made of wooden matchsticks, and a bottle containing a scene of a ship in port.

Painting by an Italian detainee given to Freda Cervelli

Matchstick jewelry box made by an Italian detainee
and given to Freda Cervelli

**Ship in port in a bottle made by an Italian detainee
and given to Freda Cervelli
The inscription reads "Fort Missoula – 4-6-1942."**

Mario loved Notre Dame football, which the Italians, no doubt, had a difficult time understanding. The games were broadcast on NBC Radio each Saturday during the fall, and Mario listened to the games as he and his newfound friends cooked at St. John's Hospital. November 27, 1943, was a particularly disappointing day for Mario as he worked in the kitchen and translated. The week before, the Fighting Irish had won a hard-fought battle over Iowa Preflight, 14–13. One game remained in the season, and Notre Dame was on the verge of being undefeated. Mario couldn't wait to hear the game, but unfortunately, that day there was no radio reception. Later that night, getting ready for bed, Mario listened to the evening news. Notre Dame had lost 19–14 in the last two minutes of the game, losing to the Great Lakes Naval Training Center, a team full of new draftees.

That year, Johnny Lujack took over calling the signals when Notre Dame's former quarterback joined the Marines. Mario wrote to Lujack personally asking for pictures and autographs. Mario received a postcard, probably from a member of the Notre Dame staff, explaining that collegiate rules prevented players from fulfilling such requests, but suggesting that Mario write to the publicity department of the school. Mario wrote a letter and sent five dollars as well, a large sum in those days, and in return received some thirty pictures of various players, as well as other Notre Dame memorabilia. Mario kept the postcard, pictures, and other items through the years. In the 1944 and 1945 football seasons, Lujack was in the Navy, but after the war, he returned to his starting position and went on to become the Heisman Trophy winner in 1947. He later played quarterback for the Chicago Bears as well.

While the challenge of the sickness and the death of his father certainly drastically changed Mario's life, he persevered through the difficulty. Despite the fact that he worked hard to provide for his mother and siblings, he began to enjoy new interests and new friendships. Mario's world grew larger.

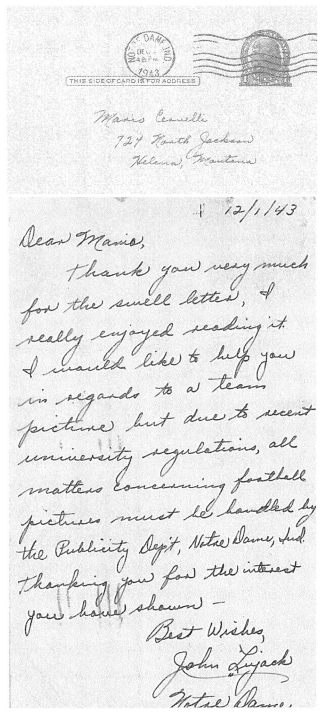

Johnny Lujack's postcard

To New York and the Army

Some time after the death of her husband, Freda received a letter from her Uncle Elia in New York telling her she should move to Ballston Lake with her family. He assured her that he could help support them and that his home was big enough. Freda eventually came to believe that relocating to New York would be best for her family and, in February, 1944, the Cervellis moved back to be with Uncle Elia. Mario quickly found work at the American Locomotive Company (ALCO), a producer of trains and, later, tanks. A few months afterward, in July, they moved to Schenectady.

Uncle Elia

Just after his eighteenth birthday, Mario walked to the Albany Street Fire Station to register for the United States draft. Three months later, in October, he received his draft notice with instructions to report to the Albany National Guard Armory for a physical examination. Classified 1-A, he took his oath of induction into the United States Army on November 10.

App. not Req.

Prepare in Duplicate

Local Board No. 318 23
Schenectady County 093

3 1944 358

7 Fire Sta., 3rd Ave. & Orchard St.
Schenectady, 3, N. Y.

(LOCAL BOARD DATE STAMP WITH CODE)

Oct. 23, 1944
(Date of mailing)

ORDER TO REPORT FOR INDUCTION

The President of the United States,

To_____ Mario_____ Bonino_____ Cervelli_____
(First name)   (Middle name)   (Last name)

Order No. 13548

GREETING:

Having submitted yourself to a local board composed of your neighbors for the purpose of determining your availability for training and service in the land or naval forces of the United States, you are hereby notified that you have now been selected for training and service therein.

You will, therefore, report to the local board named above at 512 State St., Sch'dy
Waiting Room

at 7:15 a. m., on the 10th day of November , 1944
(Hour of reporting)

This local board will furnish transportation to an induction station. You will there be examined, and, if accepted for training and service, you will then be inducted into the land or naval forces.

Persons reporting to the induction station in some instances may be rejected for physical or other reasons. It is well to keep this in mind in arranging your affairs, to prevent any undue hardship if you are rejected at the induction station. If you are employed, you should advise your employer of this notice and of the possibility that you may not be accepted at the induction station. Your employer can then be prepared to replace you if you are accepted, or to continue your employment if you are rejected.

Willful failure to report promptly to this local board at the hour and on the day named in this notice is a violation of the Selective Training and Service Act of 1940, as amended, and subjects the violator to fine and imprisonment.

If you are so far removed from your own local board that reporting in compliance with this order will be a serious hardship and you desire to report to a local board in the area of which you are now located, go immediately to that local board and make written request for transfer of your delivery for induction, taking this order with you.

Member or clerk of the local board.

U. S. GOVERNMENT PRINTING OFFICE   16—12271-5

D. S. S. Form 150
(Revised 1-15-43)

Mario's induction notice

Immediately, he and the other inductees boarded a train to report to Fort Dix, New Jersey, arriving on a Saturday. They received the necessary supplies and moved into their barracks. As they were settling in, a sergeant walked up to him and said, "Tie a towel on your bunk."

"Why?" Mario asked.

"You'll find out tomorrow," the sergeant replied.

Private First Class Mario Cervelli

Obeying orders, he did what he was told, having no idea what awaited him. The next morning at 5:00, superiors abruptly woke him from sleep and told him the towel meant that he had KP duty.

He worked the entire Sunday in the kitchen, one of only three days he stayed at Fort Dix.

Along with hundreds of others, he boarded another train, not knowing where he was going. Two days later he arrived in Birmingham, Alabama, and boarded a truck for a three-hour drive to Fort McClellan Training Center, where he spent from November to April in basic training. He then traveled to Fort Meade, Maryland, where the soldiers were issued new equipment and uniforms for their time overseas.

Throughout his entire training period, Mario maintained his strong sense of responsibility for his mother and siblings back home. While in preparation for service overseas, he received twenty-one dollars a month, of which he sent fourteen home to his family.

After a ten-day furlough, during which he returned home to Schenectady, Mario, along with hundreds of soldiers, boarded a train from Fort Meade, again with no knowledge of where they were going. They arrived at a desolate place which no one could identify and, that evening, boarded a ship. Kept below deck until the next morning, the soldiers shared rumors as to where they were going. Once out in the open seas, at the command of their superiors, the soldiers climbed up to the deck, but they received no further information. After three more days, the military finally distributed Italian–English dictionaries, which suggested where they were headed. While others didn't know what to think, Mario was filled with joy and sentimentality, because he was on his way home. The war meant little to him at the time because he knew so little about it.

After a few more days, they arrived in Naples, Italy. Only hours later, they climbed onto trucks which took them to a big replacement depot north of Naples, where many U.S. personnel began their service in Europe. They lived in pyramid tents, eight to a tent, received instruction on different weapons, and took training hikes. Heading overseas also meant a pay increase of four dollars a month. Mario's commitment to his family didn't change; the majority of his check was sent back home.

A few weeks after they arrived, they got their first pass. They decided to head to Santa Maria, a town a few miles away. Standing by the side of the road to hitchhike, he and a few of his buddies waited a few minutes before a truck approached. "Hey, you bloody Yanks," a *Limey,* or British soldier, yelled, "want a ride?" They quickly jumped in the back of the truck.

One of the activities the young soldiers hoped to accomplish while in Santa Maria was to have their photographs taken so they could send them back to their families. They spotted an enterprising photographer ready to capitalize on such an opportunity. The photographer had set up a motorcycle and backdrop in front of his camera and was taking individual pictures of soldiers on the bike. Mario and his friends decided to all gather around the bike to take a group photo to send home.

Mario with his Army buddies

In May, 1945, they left in trucks for northern Italy. Arriving at another camp outside of Modena, he transferred into the headquarters company of the 141st Anti-Aircraft Guns and started training again for the front. For Mario, it was all an adventure; only later did he realize how young he and the others were—too young to understand the complexities of war.

In the meantime, at the war front, the fighting came to an end. Benito Mussolini, the all-powerful dictator of Italy to whom Mario had pledged allegiance earlier in his life, had later aligned himself with Adolf Hitler's Germany, declaring war on Russia and eventually on the United States. Mussolini stayed in power until July 25, 1943, when after several military defeats, most of Mussolini's colleagues turned against him at a meeting of the Fascist Grand Council. The King of Italy then dismissed and arrested him.

Benito Mussolini and Adolf Hitler, June, 1940

Several months later, Germany rescued Mussolini and made him a leader, perhaps more a puppet, of the German Army in northern Italy. Just before Allied Forces reached Milan, Mussolini tried to escape to Switzerland along with his mistress Clara Petacci, but Italian partisans caught him. The partisans executed them and fifteen others on April 28, 1945, and brought their bodies to Milan, where a mob strung up Mussolini, his mistress, and five others by their feet from the girders of an Esso gas station.

When Adolf Hitler heard what had happened, he vowed that no one would do that to him. Two days later, he and his mistress turned wife, Eva Braun, whom he had married the day before, committed suicide. Following instructions that Hitler had left, soldiers immediately burned his body.

The war in Europe soon ended and soldiers celebrated VE Day, Victory in Europe Day, on May 8, 1945. After all the military training and preparation, Mario never participated in the actual fighting. Mario and his fellow soldiers got back on trucks and rode south for three days to Rome. Along the way, the Italians encouraged celebrations of all kinds. One night as they stopped by the sea, fishermen invited the American soldiers onto their boats for wine.

Back outside of Rome, Mario settled into his new barracks in a military camp that Mussolini had built for his army. At the close of the war, Allied troops captured many enemy vehicles and kept them in a motor pool of sorts at the camp.

When he first arrived, Mario described himself as a truck driver, having delivered milk back in Helena. Now in D Company, a small weapons company, an examiner took him for his first test drive. Attempting to demonstrate his abilities, he ended up grinding the gears. "You have to double clutch these things," the examiner told him. Mario had no idea what he was talking about.

Although eventually trained to drive larger trucks as well, Mario spent most of his time driving Jeeps. Because of his ability to speak Italian fluently, Mario became a driver for "the brass," taking officers to Rome, some five miles away, dropping them off and waiting around until they were ready to return.

Mario and his Jeep (Notice his name above the grill of the Jeep).

With the fighting over, many soldiers simply waited around to be shipped home. They passed their time playing cards, hanging out in local bars, and visiting local attractions, all without much military regulation. Mario stayed in Rome from May to September.

After the war, the black market quickly emerged. The Allied Armies possessed an abundance of captured supplies that were intended for war, such as military vehicles, gasoline, tires, guns, and ammunition. They also seized day-to-day items such as cigarettes and food staples like sugar, salt and flour. After years of war, the people of Italy had very few supplies, so many of the motor pool personnel sold items to the Italians on the black market. Soldiers would, for example, put a five-gallon container full of gasoline on the back of their Jeep, drive to a nearby community, pull up to the back door of a house and honk twice. One Italian man would quickly come out and take the gasoline and another would give the soldiers twenty dollars.

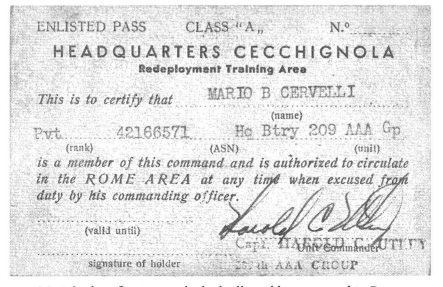

Mario's identification card which allowed him to travel in Rome

Mario saw a further example of such supplies intended for war in September of 1945. He was shipped to Tarvisio and moved into the 88th Infantry Division as part of the occupation forces. He recalls going through Pisa and seeing lines and lines of Jeeps, planned for use by the U. S. Army, all still crated in wooden boxes.

Map of Italy

One weekend in 1945, Mario traveled to the coastal city of Trieste on a pass. While there, he went to the port to see the regal ship that had brought him to America as a ten-year-old boy. By this time, however, the Rex had been stripped of its majesty. After the ship had come under control of the Germans, the British Royal Air Force attacked the Rex on September 8, 1944, and it sank, rolling onto its side in shallow water. Seeing the ship sticking out of the sea, Mario reflected back to the luxury liner's glory days and his trip to America. The ship was later broken up, removed, and scrapped, starting in 1947.

The Rex in the harbor of Trieste

Another time, Mario met Primo Carnera, a world-famous boxer and former heavy-weight champion of the world, who did most of his boxing in America. At a hotel in Rome one night, Mario encountered Carnera and got his autograph.

Mario never forgot Temu and longed to return to his birthplace. He thought his opportunity had arrived when one of his sergeants married an Italian woman and Mario was assigned to drive the new couple to her hometown north of Rome. While there for three days, Mario begged the officer to let him go to Temu, further north. His sergeant, however, refused, saying that they were at the northern limits of the Allied Forces and he couldn't guarantee safety for a lone American soldier in a Jeep running around in northern Italy.

Finally, Mario went to his commanding officer, told him the story of his early years and asked if he might be given a pass to go see his relatives in Temu. The officer consented. Mario and a friend left Rome in a Jeep and traveled to Brescia, in northern Italy. From there Mario caught a train to Edolo. Train trips after the war proved difficult because, as the Germans retreated, they blew up each bridge behind them. In the early days following the war, trains traveled from bridge to bridge. Passengers disembarked carrying their luggage, crossed the river, usually on foot, and boarded another train on the other side.

From Edolo, Mario rode a bus to Temu, arriving at midnight. He walked up the main street to the large fountain in the town square, and took a drink with his cupped hands. Not knowing where his aunt lived, he was considering what he should do next when a young man came up to him. The young Italian recognized Mario immediately because of his United States Army uniform.

Mario's aunt, Zia Seconda, had spread word throughout Temu that her nephew, an American soldier, would be coming home.

The young Italian directed Mario to his aunt's home. She still resided in the same place she had lived when he left as a ten-year-old boy. He went to the house and Zia enthusiastically welcomed him, despite the late hour.

The following day was Sunday and the day of the annual celebration of St. Bartholomew, the patron saint of Temu. Mario went to church and later to the big town feast with his Uncle Primo, who proudly introduced his nephew to the townspeople. Many of the people who lived in Temu when he left some nine years earlier were still there. Primo's pride went beyond mere family ties. His nephew had been a part of the Allied Forces that had helped liberate Italy.

Mario with his cousins from the Pasina family in Temu in August, 1945
Back row: Pierra, Mario, Bonina
Front row: Franca, Elia

Mario went home to reconnect with his family and see his hometown, but he had another purpose as well. Over the years, Mario never forgot the goodness of the owners of the local grocery store who had extended credit to his mother when she couldn't pay. Neither did he forget the promise his mother made to the woman at the grocery store as they left, nine years earlier—that somehow she would pay them back the money she owed them. Mario had come home to make good on his mother's promise. Walking purposefully to the grocery store that had allowed his family to charge food staples during their most difficult days, he paid the debt in full.

Author Joseph Conrad once wrote, "...you can't, in sound morals, condemn a man for taking care of his own integrity. It is his clear duty." Mario took care of his integrity, as well as that of his family, in keeping the promise.

Temu, 1946

Mario stayed with his family for two weeks and then went back by bus to Milan, where he stayed with his cousin Bonino and Bonino's mother. Later, he boarded a train to Rome, a trip that took two days and a night because of poor track conditions.

Mario served a couple of months longer outside of Rome and then completed his tour of duty in Tarvisio, Italy. The night before he was to leave, he received notice to report to his commanding officer. The officer said, "Cervelli, I think you should sign up for a four-year hitch."

"Why?" Mario asked.

"Because things are going to get better," came the reply.

"Why?" Mario asked again.

"Because we're going to be here a long time," the captain replied.

"Sir," Mario responded, "I just want to go home."

"Well," said the captain, "we hate to see you leave."

When the time came for departure, the troops traveled by truck to Naples, where they boarded a liberty ship bound for New York. On the trip home, they sailed through the Strait of Gibraltar and on to Casablanca. There they picked up many war brides whose soldier husbands had already returned to America. The brides had been left behind because of passport problems. Two days outside of Casablanca, the ship broke down, and they drifted west for two days, finally making it to the Azores, where they waited for three days for repairs.

Arriving in New York, the returning soldiers disembarked and were immediately transported to Fort Meade, where they waited for a couple of days before going back to Fort Dix for their discharge papers in November, 1946.

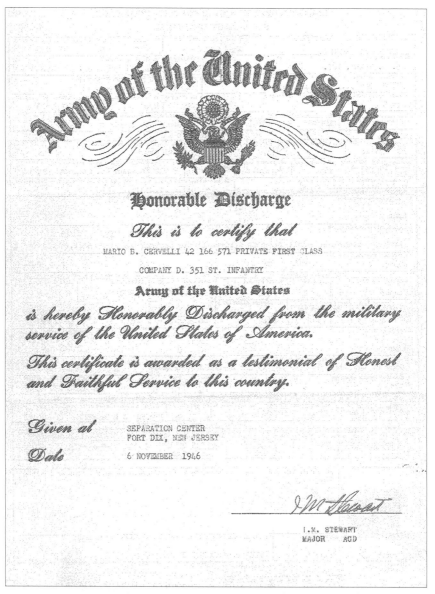

Army discharge certificate

ENLISTED RECORD AND REPORT OF SEPARATION

HONORABLE DISCHARGE

1. LAST NAME - FIRST NAME - MIDDLE INITIAL		2. ARMY SERIAL NO.	3. GRADE	4. ARM OR SERVICE	5. COMPONENT
CERVELLI, MARIO R.		42 166 571	Pfc 13Feb46	INF	AUS
6. ORGANIZATION			7. DATE OF SEPARATION	8. PLACE OF SEPARATION	
Co. D. 351st. Inf.			6 Nov 46	SEP CTR FORT DIX, NEW JERSEY	
9. PERMANENT ADDRESS FOR MAILING PURPOSES			10. DATE OF BIRTH	11. PLACE OF BIRTH	
939 Strong St., Schenectady, NY			13 Jul 6	Temo. Italy	
12. ADDRESS FROM WHICH EMPLOYMENT WILL BE SOUGHT		13. COLOR EYES	14. COLOR HAIR	15. HEIGHT	16. WEIGHT	17. NO. DEPENS.
See 9		Brn	Brn	5-7	140 LBS.	3
18. RACE	19. MARITAL STATUS	20. U.S. CITIZEN	21. CIVILIAN OCCUPATION AND NO.		
WHITE X NEGRO OTHER (specify) SINGLE X MARRIED OTHER (specify)		YES X NO	Student HS (X-02)		

MILITARY HISTORY

22. DATE OF INDUCTION	23. DATE OF ENLISTMENT	24. DATE OF ENTRY INTO ACTIVE SERVICE	25. PLACE OF ENTRY INTO SERVICE
10 Nov 44		10 Nov 44	Albany NY

SELECTIVE SERVICE DATA	26. REGISTERED YES X NO	27. LOCAL S.S.BOARD NO. 358	28. COUNTY AND STATE Schenectady N Y	29. HOME ADDRESS AT TIME OF ENTRY INTO SERVICE 932 Pleasant St. Schenectady, NY

30. MILITARY OCCUPATIONAL SPECIALTY AND NO.	31. MILITARY QUALIFICATION AND DATE (i.e., infantry, aviation and marksmanship badges, etc.)
Truck Driver Light (345)	M-1 Rifle Marksman, 148 23 Dec 44

32. BATTLES AND CAMPAIGNS

None

33. DECORATIONS AND CITATIONS   Victory Medal

Army of Occupation Medal, European African Middle Eastern Campaign Medal, World War II

34. WOUNDS RECEIVED IN ACTION

N one

35. LATEST IMMUNIZATION DATES				36.	SERVICE OUTSIDE CONTINENTAL U.S. AND RETURN		
SMALLPOX	TYPHOID	TETANUS	OTHER (specify)		DATE OF DEPARTURE	DESTINATION	DATE OF ARRIVAL
Dec 45	Dec 45	Dec 45	None		28 Mar 45	MTO	8 Apr 45

37. TOTAL LENGTH OF SERVICE				38. HIGHEST GRADE HELD			
CONTINENTAL SERVICE		FOREIGN SERVICE					
YEARS 0	MONTHS 6	DAYS 13	YEARS 1	MONTHS 5	DAYS 14	Pfc	26 Aug 46	US	11 Sep 46

39. PRIOR SERVICE

None

40. REASON AND AUTHORITY FOR SEPARATION

Conv of the Govt AR 615-365 15 Dec 44 and RR 1-1 Demob

41. SERVICE SCHOOLS ATTENDED		42. EDUCATION (Years)		
None		Grammar 8	High School 1	College 0

PAY DATA

43. LONGEVITY FOR PAY PURPOSES			44. MUSTERING OUT PAY		45. SOLDIER DEPOSITS	46. TRAVEL PAY	47. TOTAL AMOUNT, NAME OF DISBURSING OFFICER
YEARS 11	MONTHS 2	DAYS 7	TOTAL $ 300	THIS PAYMENT $ 100	None	$ 11.90	179.50 J M BARRETTE LT COL FD

INSURANCE NOTICE   137.75

IMPORTANT	IF PREMIUM IS NOT PAID WHEN DUE OR WITHIN THIRTY-ONE DAYS THEREAFTER, INSURANCE WILL LAPSE. MAKE CHECKS OR MONEY ORDERS PAYABLE TO THE TREASURER OF THE U.S. AND FORWARD TO COLLECTIONS SUBDIVISION, VETERANS ADMINISTRATION, WASHINGTON 25, D.C				

48. KIND OF INSURANCE	49. HOW PAID		50. Effective Date of Allotment Discontinuance	51. Date of Next Premium Due (One month after 30)	52. PREMIUM DUE EACH MONTH	53. INTENTION OF VETERAN TO
Nat. Serv. X	U.S. Govt.	None	Allotment X Direct to V. A.	31 Oct 46	30 Nov 46	$ 6.40	Continue X Continue Only Discontinue

54.	55. REMARKS (This space for completion of above items or entry of other items specified in W. D. Directives)
RIGHT THUMB PRINT	LAPEL BUTTON ISSUED NO DAYS LOST UNDER AW 107 ASRSCORE (2 SEP 45) 16

56. SIGNATURE OF PERSON BEING SEPARATED	57. PERSONNEL OFFICER (Type name, grade and organization - signature)
Mario B. Cervelli	VIVA M. WICKERSHEIM, 1ST. LT. FA

WD AGO FORM 53 - 55   This form supersedes all previous editions of
1 November 1944   WD AGO Forms 53 and 55 for enlisted persons
                         entitled to an Honorable Discharge, which
                         will not be used after receipt of this revision.

Army discharge paper

MARIO B. CERVELLI

To you who answered the call of your country and served in its Armed Forces to bring about the total defeat of the enemy, I extend the heartfelt thanks of a grateful Nation. As one of the Nation's finest, you undertook the most severe task one can be called upon to perform. Because you demonstrated the fortitude, resourcefulness and calm judgment necessary to carry out that task, we now look to you for leadership and example in further exalting our country in peace.

Harry Truman

THE WHITE HOUSE

Thank you letter from President Harry Truman

Mario went back home to Schenectady, arriving at 11:00 a.m. He changed out of his uniform and walked back to ALCO to see if he still had a job. He went back to work the next day.

Mario with ALCO restaurant workers in 1947

Mario lived with his family in Schenectady until 1949, his sister and brother graduating from high school there. Mario worked the whole time for ALCO, and Freda provided housekeeping for a local hotel.

As difficult as the war was for the entire world, Mario recalls his days in the United States Army as some of the best days of his life. Due to his father's reaction to Mussolini's dictatorship, Mario left his homeland but warmly adopted his new country. Despite family hardships, he embraced the freedoms and opportunities the United States provided. He was proud to have served his adopted country in the country of his birth.

Back to Montana

In the hot August of 1948, Mario boarded a sweltering bus, traveled to Montana, and vacationed alone back in Helena. Construction of the new Canyon Ferry Dam, located some seventeen miles east of Helena, provided many employment opportunities, and friends tried to convince him to return. Mario considered the prospect but went back to New York to his ALCO job.

A year later, the family decided the time was right to move back to Montana. They packed up their 1947 Mercury sedan and drove all the way to Helena. Having no place to live, they stayed at a 6th and Ewing hotel and later bought a home at 100 Chaucer. Mario found work at the Helena Bottling Company in October, 1949, dispensing Nesbitt's Orange, Tang Root Beer, Squirt, and soda water. After being laid off the following spring, a friend of the family, a lady for whom he had caddied at Pine Hills Golf Course, told him to go to the Kessler Brewing Company, where he began working in May, 1950.

Freda worked three days a week doing housekeeping. She went to work for her friends, the family of Art Nelson, a vice president of the First National Bank, and the family of Sherman Smith, an attorney. Mario had caddied for the Nelsons and the Smiths as a thirteen-year-old boy.

Loyal friendships had become a constant theme of the Cervelli family. After they had said good-bye to their Helena friends and moved to Ballston Lake, after Mario served in the Army, after Mario returned to Schenectady for several years, and after the Cervellis finally moved back to Helena in 1949, Freda went to work for her friends. The Cervellis' friendships remained strong.

Afterword

This book has focused on the years of Mario's life leading up to his permanent residency in Helena at the age of twenty-three. Throughout these years, he had overcome many obstacles and sought, as Joseph Conrad said, to take care of his integrity.

Later, Mario moved again, with his sister and mother, to 523 North Ewing, a house the three purchased together. He continued to support his mother. When asked how long he supported Freda, he replied, "I didn't keep a whole paycheck until I was thirty years old."

He continued to live with his mother until May 19, 1956, when he married Janet Bader. Initially he and Janet established a home at 946 Breckenridge; later, they lived at 1704 Hollins, then 1459 Wilder, and finally resided for many years at 615 North Rodney. They had four children—Nina, Jim, Lisa, and Natalie.

Mario and Janet divorced in 1981, and Mario moved into his long-term residence, his former mother-in-law's mobile home, at 1805 Joslyn, trailer number 156.

Mario worked for the Kessler Brewing Company until 1958, when the brewery closed. He continued driving delivery trucks full-time from 1958 until 1988 and then part-time from 1988 until 1991, when he retired.

Freda Cervelli

Freda worked as a housekeeper until she retired in her seventies. She died on January 26, 1994, at the age of ninety-one, having lived over fifty-two years as a widow. She was buried next to her husband, Cesare, at Resurrection Cemetery in Helena.

DEATHS

Saturday, Jan. 29, 1994

Freda Cervelli

Freda Cervelli, 91, died Wednesay, Jan. 26, 1994, at her daughter's home.

Freda was born in Temu, Italy on Jan. 20, 1903. She came to the United States with her three children to join her husband, Cesare, in 1936.

Freda worked hard all of her life, mostly as a housekeeper. Following the death of her husband in 1941, she moved with her family to New York to be near relatives. They returned to Helena to stay in 1949.

Freda was a life-long member of St. Helena Cathedral. She enjoyed working in her yard and caring for her children and grandchildren.

She was preceded in death by a brother and sister, her husband, and a grandson Larry.

Survivors include a sister in Milan, Italy; a daughter, Frances Shull of Helena; and sons, Mario Cervelli of Helena and Dino Cervelli of Sonora, Calif.; grandchildren, Nina Johnson, Jim Cervelli, Lisa Routzhan, Natalie Cervelli, Richard, Bill and Dan Shull, Mary Carter, Bruce Cervelli and Kathy O'Hagen; 13 grandchildren and numerous nieces and nephews in Italy.

The family will receive friends on Sunday from 1 to 2 p.m. during visitation at the Retz Funreal Home. Mass of the resurrection will be celebrated Monday, Jan. 31, at 10 a.m. in the St. Helena Cathedral with Rev. John Darragh as celebrant. The commital services will follow at Resurrection Cemetery.

Memorials may be given to St. Helena Cathedral or Hospice of St. Peter's Hospital.

Freda Cervelli's obituary

Source: *Independent Record*, Helena, Montana, January 29, 1994

The Cervellis' gravestones in Resurrection Cemetery

Freda Cervelli's gravestone

Cesare Cervelli's gravestone

Mario's sister Frances married William Shull and had four children—Dick, Mary, Bill, and Dan. They resided in Plains, Montana, for many years before she and William divorced. She now lives in Helena, just a block away from Mario.

Mario's brother Dino spent most of his life in Stockton, Sacramento, and Sonora, California. He married Doris "Cookie" Cartwright and had three children—Kathy, Bruno, and Larry. After their divorce, he married Carol Burns. He died in 2000, and his family members spread his ashes in the mountains of Montana.

In 2007, Mario read a brief article in the Helena newspaper about a new museum at Fort Missoula to remember the internment of Italians and others during World War II. Mario immediately knew what he wanted to do and called to talk to the curator. Then, traveling to Missoula, he brought the German shepherd painting, the bottle containing a scene of a ship in port, and the matchstick box back home to the Fort, donating them to the museum and sharing his story.

Since 1979, Mario has returned to Italy several times to visit his family, many of whom still live in Temu.

Mario on the ranch, July, 2009

So perhaps Booker T. Washington summed up Mario's early years best when he said, "…success is to be measured not so much by the position that one has reached in life as by the obstacles which he has overcome while trying to succeed."

Mario is not a perfect man, nor is his story a perfect story. Early in Mario's life in Temu and Helena, however, he learned the value of hard work. He understood the importance of family and community. He became thankful for even small pleasures. He fully appreciated the significance of loyalty, respect, and integrity. Mario has sought to live out these values.

About the Author

Keith Johnson's fondness for stories inspired him to preserve these treasures for his family in the United States and Italy, and for the people of Montana. Keith has been a pastor in Bumba, Congo, and in Helena, Montana, where he currently lives with his wife and two daughters.